A BRIEF HISTORY OF
PRINTING AND PUBLISHING IN IRELAND

A Brief History of Printing and Publishing in Ireland

by Vincent Kinane

NATIONAL PRINT MUSEUM
DUBLIN

Published in 2002 by The National Print Museum, Dublin, Ireland
as a limited edition of 950 copies.

ISBN 0–9543799–0–X

Designed and set Monotype hot metal at The National Print Museum
Plates by M&W Graphics
Printed letterpress at T. S. Connolly Ltd.
on Huntsman Velvet 130gm paper sponsored by Robert Horne Group
Binding by Duffy Bookbinders

Dedicated to the memory of
Vincent Kinane

Johann Gutenberg (1400–1468) the inventor of moveable type. Some lines from his famous *Bible* are shown below.

Audi fili mi disciplinā p̄ris tui et ne dimittas legem m̄ris tue:ut addatur gracia rapiti tuo:⁊ torques collo tuo. fili mi si te lactauerint p̄c̄ores:ne acquiescas eis. Si dixerit veni nobiscū·

The Sixteenth
and
Seventeenth Centuries

PRINTING WAS A LATE ARRIVAL in Ireland. A century after Johann Gutenberg's invention of the process in Mainz it was introduced by the government for administrative and propaganda purposes. Humphrey Powell (fl. 1548–1567) was sent over from London to Dublin and in 1551 he finished his first book, *The Boke of Common Praier*. The first book using the Irish character, *Aibidil Gaoidheilge agus Caiticiosma*, was printed in 1571 by an unidentified printer. Until the 1640s there was never more than one press in operation in the country at any one time. The output was small – a handful of mostly official books and proclamations.

Whereas in England control of the press was vested in the Company of Stationers, in Ireland the King's Printer's patent served this purpose. The patent gave a monopoly to the holder over all printing, bookselling and bookbinding in the country. The first patent came into force in 1604, and in theory, except for a short period in the 1640s, this monopoly held until 1732. The reality was a bit more complicated.

In 1618 the London Stationers' Company was granted the King's Printer's patent in Ireland. It set up a printing house in Dublin and serviced its bookselling needs in Ireland from a

¶ A prayer for the Lord Deputie, (to be saied)
betwene the two last Collectes of the Latenie.

Oft mercifull and euerlaftyng God, whiche a=
mongeſt other thy ſundrie and manifold giftes,
(by geuyng of good and rightuous miniſters in
earth) dooeſt declare thy fauourable mercie and
excedyng goodneſſe: We moſt humblie beſeche
thee, that thou wilt ſo lighten the herte of thy ſeruaunt (Sir
James Croft) now gouernour ouer this realme, vnder our
moſt dread and ſoueraigne Lord, Edwarde the firſt: that he
maie by the might of thy power, gouerne and guide the ſame
in thy moſt holy lawes: grauntyng hym grace (by pureneſſe
of life and feruent zeale to thy trueth) to be an example to all
other, to leaue of their olde abhominable errours: And that
he maie (hauyng ſtedfaſt confidence in thy helpe) not onely
bring the people to liue in thy feare, and due obedience to their
kyng: but alſo by miniſtring of Juſtice, may kepe them from
their accuſtomed, moſt frowarde and diueliſhe ſeditions, in
reſt, peace and quietneſſe. And graunt Lord we beſeche thee,
for thy ſonne Jeſus Chriſtes ſake, that through thee he be de=
fended from the priuie craftes of thoſe, whiche ſhall go about
maliciouſly to let or hyndre his good and godly procedynges:
and that his dooynges alwaies and in all thynges, maie
tende to thy glorie, the kynges honour, and the common
wealth of this lande. That thou wilte helpe hym,
mainteyne hym, ſtrengthen him, in thy waies di=
rect hym, and appoinct iuſt and faithfull dea=
lyng officers and ſeruauntes about hym,
we moſt humblie praie thee good lord:
who with thy ſonne and the holy
ghoſt, liueſt and reigneſt,
worlde without
ende. A=
men.

Page from the *Book of Common Prayer*, 1551.

8

warehouse in London. The venture did not prove a success and in 1639 the Irish Stock, as it was called, was sold to William Bladen. In the 1640s the King's Printer's monopoly was curtailed to government printing only, and as a consequence a few other presses were established in Dublin and in the provinces.

In the troubled 1640s the propaganda needs of the warring factions of King, Parliament and Confederate Catholics led to presses being set up in the provinces. The first to appear was in

22 **URRNAJĠHCHE.**

óóćuʃ aʃ aʃ nʒnȟoṁaʃʃċuȷƀ ƒén,nóas
aʃ oċuȷȽȼeanaʃ,aċo aʃ oo ċʃócaȷʃe ʃo
ṁóȷʃʃe,oo ʃéʃ mq oo ʒeallȽ ȼú aʃ nʒuȷ
ƀe óéȷʃoeacho , ȝ na hȷaʃʃaȼuȷʃ oo nȷ
mɷȷo oȥȼ oo ȼaƀaȷʃȼ oúȷň,an aȷnm oo
ℿȟȷcȷóṁuȷJoʃaCʃȷoʃo aʃ Oȼȷʒeq-
ɔa. ℿeoć ȼuʒaȷȼhne óúȷň, ʃň ƒén, oo-
ćʃuňȷuʒaó ȝ oo ȼȷonol aʒcȼaň aćéle,
na aȷnmʃén,lé lán ʒeallaó oeaʃƀȼa, ʒo
mbȷaȼ ʃé ƒén, naʃ meaʃʒ, ȝ naʃ mea-
óón, ȝ nȷ he ʃn aṁáȷn ,aċo ʒo mbȷaȼh
ʃé aʒaȷno,maʃ aȷóne aʒus maʃ ȼeaćou
ʃe oo ȼáoƀ oo cũaćoʃa, oʃaʒaȷl oúȷň
ʒaċ uȷle nȼ̇ȼe oá bʃaȷcʃʃó ʃé oo o choȷl
ƀeaňuȷʒ̇ȼeʃe ȷn ȼuʒȼa o'aʃ ʃȷacoanas
leaʃ.Uȷme ʃȷ aȼámɷȷo ʒuo ʒȝóe aʒuʃ

From *Aibidil Gaoidheilge & Caiticiosma,* by John O'Kearney.
The first type specially cut for the printing of Irish. Made to the order of Queen Elizabeth in 1571 for the instruction of the Irish people in the Protestant religion.

Waterford in 1643, Thomas Bourke being the printer. (A 'Waterford 1555' imprint exists but it proves to be false, having been printed in Emden in the Netherlands). Kilkenny was the second provincial city to have a printing press. In 1645 printing equipment was imported from France by the Jesuits and their first imprint appeared in 1646.

Peter de Pienne was printing for the Confederate Catholics in Waterford in 1647, but turned up to produce the first Cork imprint in 1648, this time for the Royalists. In 1649 Cork was captured by Commonwealth troops and the press used for Parliamentary propaganda. The Cork press was the only one to survive closure under the Commonwealth in the 1650s. The sole other town to have a press in the seventeenth century was Belfast, established by Patrick Neill and James Blow; their first imprint appeared in 1694. There is also evidence that an itinerant press was attached to the army of William III circa 1690 but so far none of its output has been identified.

The King's Printer's full monopoly was reimposed at the Restoration in 1660. Although nominally the patentee had control over every aspect of the book trades – printing, bookselling, bookbinding – in reality printing was the one most jealously guarded. In 1673 John Crooke, the holder, successfully challenged a rival press, run by William Bladen's heirs, and had its equipment confiscated.

In 1670 the few stationer/booksellers working in Dublin, presumably under licence from the King's Printer, joined with the cutlers and the painter-stainers to found the Guild of St. Luke the Evangelist. Its charter allowed only members of the Guild, properly trained, to carry on book trades in the capital. Full membership was reserved for Protestants, but Catholics could become 'quarter brothers', paying stiff fees on a quarterly basis. Although the Guild continued in existence until 1841 it never really became a regulatory force. By the early decades of the eighteenth century it had become little more than a political club, whereby full members could become freemen of the City with voting rights to the Corporation.

The monopoly afforded the King's Printer inhibited the emergence of specialist booksellers. General wholesale merchants conducted the importation and distribution of books. Dublin naturally dominated the bookselling trade, taking roughly 75 per cent of all imports. But there was a considerable trade, shipped through Bristol and Chester, to ports along the south and west coasts – Waterford, Cork, Limerick, Galway. Religious works and schoolbooks were the staples. There is evidence at the end of the century that only 20 per cent of the books in circulation were printed in Ireland; about 75 per cent were imports from England, and the remaining 5 per cent came from the continent. As a consequence books were expensive in Ireland, importation costs adding about 25 per cent to retail prices.

The overall quality of printing in the seventeenth century was very poor. Bishop Edward Wetenhall had to apologise in the following terms in the preface to his *Of Gifts and Offices in the Public Worship of God,* printed by Benjamin Tooke in 1678: 'every mans eye will inform him, that the Character which the Printer had to use, being somewhat old and worn, there are several letters and syllables very blind, or scarce appearing, some not at all...Had the Press here more encouragement, it would be better furnished.'

However changes were already underway. The relative peace in the country in the latter part of the century led to a growing demand for printing. The King's Printer's inability to keep up with this demand was an argument used by Joseph Ray (d. 1709), printer and bookseller in Dublin, when he challenged the patentee's monopoly before the Lord Lieutenant in 1680–1681. He was supported in his cause by the Guild. Although the verdict went against Ray, the monopoly was in practice broken. Ray continued to print unchallenged and in 1681 was the first appointee to the office of Printer to the City of Dublin. A rapid expansion of the printing and book trades was underway, an expansion which would reach its fullest expression in the eighteenth century.

A typical printing press of the seventeenth century.

The Eighteenth Century

THE British Copyright Act of 1709 did not extend to Ireland, and so reprints of London publications became the staple of the Dublin book trade. These reprints, legitimate under Irish law, were cheaper than the originals. The English booksellers naturally objected to this, since, after North America, Ireland was their biggest export market. In 1739 the Copyright Act was reinforced by the Importation Act whereby it became illegal to import into Britain any reprint of a book first printed there. The existence of many Dublin-printed books with false London imprints – 'A. Moore', 'Web', 'T. Cooper' were favoured names – appears to indicate an intention of smuggling into Britain to circumvent this law. But it would seem that smuggling (with false imprints or otherwise) was not on the huge scale that the London booksellers claimed. In fact in many cases payment for reprints was made to the English copyright holder. Many false London imprints may well have been aimed at the fashion conscious Irish reader (and later the American reader when North America became a valuable export market) who wanted a 'London' printed book.

Lack of legislation to protect property in Ireland meant that many Irish authors turned to London for publication of their works. Wider distribution networks from there, as well as the reputation attached to London imprints, were other factors, and continue to be so even today. James Arbuckle summed up the attitude in the 1720s when he wrote that the work of Irish authors 'received no attention unless it be made authentic by being printed in London.' Because of the lack of copyright protection in Ireland for their publications, the booksellers

13

assumed that authors could not claim any legal property either. This assumption was challenged in the courts in 1787 by William Wilson, who claimed that material in his *Post-Chaise Companion* had been pirated by the press corrector Richard Lewis. Wilson won, thus establishing a precedent for literary property in the country, but the implications never seem to have been realised by authors.

Arbuckle in the 1720s also recorded the new confidence in the Dublin book trade: 'We have fallen into the way of reprinting several valuable books, which we formerly used to pay great rates for from abroad; and have given editions of some of the classicks, which deserve great commendation.' The classics to which he refers were those edited by Constantia Grierson, which were printed by her husband George (c. 1680–1753), the first of a family dynasty to hold the King's Printer patent. Another manifestation of this burgeoning confidence was the foundation of the Dublin University Press in 1734, which survives today and is the oldest printing and publishing house in Ireland.

Constantia Grierson may have been the author of *A Poem on the Art of Printing,* printed as a broadsheet in 1728 on a printing press mounted on a cart and distributed free to spectators during the Riding of the Franchises. This vestige of mediaeval pageantry was a triennial festival during which the Corporation paraded around the boundaries of the city. The expense to each guild was considerable, so much so that on occasion the stationers refused to take part.

In the absence of an Irish copyright law, publication in Dublin was regulated by an informal agreement among the booksellers whereby whoever first posted up or published his intentions to bring out a certain work, secured the rights in it. Inevitably there were disputes and rival editions – notably over Alexander Pope's *Dunciad* (1729) and Samuel Richardson's *Sir Charles Grandison* (1753) – but on the whole the system worked well.

If titles were judged to have a good potential market individual booksellers would undertake to have them printed. For books with a more doubtful market or if greater investment was needed proposals might be issued to have them printed by subscription. The work would be put to press when a few hundred copies had been subscribed for, thus sharing the risk. In the 1770s the booksellers often formed themselves into loose partnerships, styled the Company of Booksellers, to finance works. The Company also regulated imports from London, where John Murray acted as its agent. The concept of a specialist wholesale bookseller, supplying the trade at discount – a publisher in effect as we understand it today – began to emerge at the end of the century. This was the direction which Luke White (–1775- d.1824), one of the largest Dublin booksellers, was taking at the end of the century.

Besides making books available in their shops, booksellers also advertised their stocks through newspapers and individual catalogues. Comprehensive catalogues, containing several thousand books from a range of booksellers, was a new departure of the last quarter of the century. The first appeared in 1774 and the last in 1791. They became known as *The Dublin Catalogue of Books* and were aimed at the bookseller or individual in the country.

The printer/bookseller predominated in the Dublin trade, unlike London where the roles of printer and bookseller were strictly demarcated. George Faulkner (1700–1775), printer to Jonathan Swift and proprietor of the *Dublin Journal,* styled

Title page from *The Works of Jonathan Swift* printed in Dublin 1774.

'Prince of Dublin Printers' by Lord Chesterfield, was the supreme example of the printer/bookseller. Samuel Powell (–1728–d.1775) was the largest of the few specialist printers. He was sufficiently wealthy to build a large printing house in Dame Street in 1762, this at a time when most printing shops were stuck in a few rooms in someone's house or behind a retail shop. Over the century the growth in the trade saw the emergence of specialist printers/booksellers, as for example Sarah Cotter in legal works, William Gilbert in medical books. Thomas Jackson in children's literature, and the printers Graisberry and Campbell, who carved a niche in academic books and printing in Irish.

The book trade served the English-speaking Protestant establishment. Catholic printing only emerged in any quantity towards the end of the century. Not that the Penal Laws were a great burden to Catholic members of the trade, as they were seldom enforced. Catholic devotional works under the Dublin imprints of Ignatius Kelly, Patrick Lord, Patrick Wogan and Richard Cross appeared throughout the century. The chapbook trade, aimed largely at the rural population, was the one area of the trade dominated by Catholic printers and booksellers. An advertisement in 1719 by a Catholic bookseller, Luke Dowling, will give a flavour of his business and stock: 'Valentines, Montelions, Reynards, Troys, Parsimus, Fortunatus, Gesta Romanorum, Wise Masters, &c. Also most sorts of prayer books, books of piety, devotion and school books, all of which the said Dowling will sell by wholesale or retail, to all country chapmen and others...'

Not much is known about the journeymen and apprentices of the master printers and booksellers. Boys started their seven-year apprenticeship in their early teens or even earlier. It was considered to be a very respectable trade and often the master charged a considerable premium, sometimes up to £100, before training began. In a general printing shop a boy might train both as a compositor and as a pressman, while an apprentice to a bookseller would learn how to run a shop and, if there was a bindery, bookbinding. As the century progressed the tendency was to specialise in one aspect of these trades. Apprentices were paid only a fraction of what a journeyman earned so there was a great temptation for masters to have a disproportionate number of boys. In 1765 it was reported that there were 116 apprentices in the Dublin printing trade, yet only 70 journeymen. This was a constant irritant to the journeymen (and was to remain so well into the nineteenth century). As early as 1773 they had formed themselves into the Amicable Society of Printers, and presented a petition on the matter to Parliament in 1780.

There was no fixed wage (establishment or 'stab wage' as it became known) for workers; journeymen were paid by the piece. In 1800, the earliest date for which we have firm evidence, compositors in Dublin were paid 4½ pence per 1,000 ens (a notional hour's work), while pressmen got 4d. for a similar notional period. The men would have been expected to work a long week, perhaps up to 72 hours. Thus in times of full employment a weekly wage of £1-7-0 could be earned by compositors, and £1-4-0 by pressmen (for comparison papermakers were earning less than 15 shillings in 1796, and binders probably less than £1). If they worked with more expedition they could earn more. In 1784 Patrick Campbell advertised for compositors to work on the *Volunteer Journal,* stating that £1-1-0 to £1-11-6 could be earned. Of course work was never that consistent; there would have been long periods of idleness with no pay.

In the early part of the century much of the equipment and supplies for the book trade had to be imported. Holland, England and Scotland were important sources for type. Paper came from Italy, Holland, France and Britain. But as the century progressed the country became more and more self-sufficient. Ralph Sadleir and later his widow Elizabeth were making type in Dublin in the early part of the century. Malone and Perry's typefoundry was established in the late 1740s, and was later run by Stephen Parker, who in 1787 advertised the first fount of irish type to be cut and cast in Ireland. James Robinson advertised in 1730 that he made printing presses, both the wooden parts and the metal screw, as did Francis Joy in Belfast in the 1740s. Local papermills, protected by tariffs on imports, tried to keep up with the expanding demand. Irish tanneries supplied calf and sheep skins for the bookbinders; only the expensive morocco and turkey skins had to be imported.

Nominally there was no government control over the output of the press. But printers were often brought before the courts under common law charged with sedition and libel. Several of Swift's printers were imprisoned for printing his barbed anonymous pamphlets. John Harding was one, and when he was released after one period of confinement in 1724, published the following verse:

Forth from my dark and dismal room
Behold to life again I'm come;
By long confinement poor John Harding
Has hardly left a single farthing.

Even George Faulkner suffered a period of incarceration. But it was the scandalous libels which appeared in the *Public Monitor*, a Dublin newspaper which appeared between 1772 and 1774, that gave the government an excuse to introduce the first statute laws to control the printing press. The first Stamp Act of 1774 imposed duties on newspapers and pamphlets, and required printers to print their names and addresses in the works published. Subsequent laws tightened the noose. By the Press Act of 1798 the names of all newspaper proprietors, printers and workmen had to be registered with the Stamp Commissioners, and each proprietor had to lodge security of £500. It was in effect a return to official licensing. The newspaper press was decimated. Whereas in the 1780s Dublin had supported 10 newspapers, by 1798 this number had been halved, and of those, three were government organs.

Because of British restrictions on exports from Ireland for much of the century the domestic market was the main outlet for the book trade. When full free trade was allowed in 1783 there was a huge increase in exports, especially to America. *Wilson's Dublin Directories* record an expansion in book trade businesses from 70 in 1781 to 118 in 1793. In the mid-1780s Dublin supported 53 printing houses. But the 1790s saw a disastrous decline, the key factor being the expense and lack of paper. The traditional French sources were cut off by war, and supplies from England and Scotland attracted heavy import duties. On top of that there was a long strike in Ireland by journeymen papermakers in 1795. The Irish mills could not keep up with the demand. There were many financial failures in the trade – including Robert Marchbank, one of its most senior figures – and a wave of key figures emigrated to America. The decline was compounded by the fact that many in the book

THE

H I S T O R Y

AND

ADVENTURES

OF THE RENOWNED

DON QUIXOTE.

TRANSLATED FROM THE SPANISH OF

MIGUEL DE CERVANTES SAAVEDRA.

TO WHICH IS PREFIXED,

SOME ACCOUNT OF THE AUTHOR'S LIFE.

BY *T. SMOLLETT*, M. D.

ORNAMENTED WITH ENGRAVINGS,

BY THE FIRST MASTERS,

FROM THE DESIGNS OF THE MADRID ROYAL ACADEMY, &c.

IN FOUR VOLUMES.

VOL. I.

DUBLIN:

JOHN CHAMBERS.

1796.

Title page of *The History and Adventures of Don Quixote*, printed by John Chambers in Dublin 1796.

21

trade were members of the United Irishmen, and were imprisoned or exiled after the 1798 Rebellion.

Beyond Dublin there were few towns that could support specialist printer/booksellers. The Blows and the Joys in Belfast, and Eugene Swiney and James Haly in Cork were exceptions. James Blow (–1694-d.1759), in association with his brother-in-law Patrick Neill, was the pioneer printer in Belfast. He specialised in religious publications, including editions of the Bible. Francis Joy (fl.1737–1748) was unique in the Irish book trade. Besides being a printer and a bookseller, he also made his own type, ink, printing presses, and paper. He founded the first Belfast news-paper, *The Belfast News-letter,* in 1737. Eugene Swiney (–1753-d.1781), proprietor of the *Cork Journal,* produced a broad range of publications, including many Catholic works. Some were very extensive: his edition of Nicholas Caussin's *Holy Court,* printed in 1765–1767, is a folio volume which runs to over 900 pages.

The well-to-do country book-buyer would have visited or corresponded with a specialist bookseller in one of the cities, who had large stocks. The poorer classes had to rely on the limited stock of the country town's general store or the itinerant pedlar. The establishment of provincial newspapers was the impetus to the spread of the printing press beyond the main cities. Newspapers provided the stability of a recurrent income for these printing offices which also served the fluctuating jobbing needs of the local community – posters, commercial stationery, handbills etc. Limerick received its first press in 1716, but Galway, strangely for such a thriving city, had to wait until 1754. Up to 1760 the most important expansions took place in the northern towns – Derry, Armagh, Newry, Downpatrick, Drogheda – but by 1800 printing presses were established in 34 provincial towns.

The Nineteenth Century

THE extension of the Copyright Act to Ireland in 1801, following the Act of Union of 1800, had a devastating effect on the Dublin printing and publishing trades. Speaking in 1821 William Wakeman, a bookseller, said that the loss of the reprint trade 'almost annihilated' the Dublin printing trade. One commentator in 1805 recorded that scarcely a dozen new titles were produced per year. The publication of books plummeted 80 per cent in the first half of the century, according to another source. John Cumming (–1808–d.1850), one of the largest printer/publishers in the city, owed his survival to his extensive contacts with British publishers. Booksellers relied heavily on the sale of imports; books imported from Great Britain increased from £7,000 in 1800 to £27,000 in 1815. The fact that the printing trade had a very poor reputation for quality deepened the depression. The London publishing house, Longman and Co., wrote in 1820 to Richard Milliken, a bookseller in Dublin, stating that it was a common opinion that it was 'almost impossible to have a handsome book printed in Dublin'. The printers who survived best were those that had government contracts, or were official printers to various societies, such as the Kildare Place Society which published huge quantities of chapbooks from 1817 onwards. Richard Coyne (–1808–d.1856), printer to St. Patrick's College, Maynooth, and Graisberry and Campbell, printer to Trinity College, had extensive jobbing business from their patron even if the amount of book work was very small.

The difficulties of the Dublin printing trade were reflected in the foundation of the Dublin Typographical Provident Society, in effect a trade union for journeymen printers, the roots of which went back into the eighteenth century. It is traditionally believed that it started in 1809, but Matthew Ryan, secretary to the DTPS, giving evidence to a parliamentary commission in 1838, stated that it was during a period of high unemployment in 1825 that the printers formed themselves into a society for their mutual benefit. During the general business slump of 1826 some printers ended up breaking stones on government outdoor relief schemes.

The local nature of the output of the provincial presses meant that they were not affected by the introduction of the Copyright Act in 1801 and the period up to 1840 was one of further expansion in the provinces. It has been estimated that 5,000 works were printed at provincial presses in the first half of the century, while the output for the whole of the eighteenth century was only 1,500. The engine that drove these provincial presses continued to be the local newspaper, but many had to be general factotums to make a living. For example John Stacy in Carrick-on-Suir was also a barber, engraver, artist and writer. Others, however, were substantial printers. Alexander Wilkinson in Newry printed works in the 1810s for publishers in Dublin, London and Edinburgh, while in Waterford Edward Bull took on similar commissions in the first quarter of the century.

The recovery of the Irish publishing trade happened slowly throughout the 1820s. A correspondent in the *Christian Examiner* in 1828 decried the slovenly printing in the few publications that came from the Dublin press, but acknowledged that this was changing. He looked forward to the future when the Irish would no longer be 'the mere retailers of English works'. The publication in 1830 of William Carleton's very popular *Traits and Stories of the Irish Peasantry* was a watershed in the revival of native publishing. It proved that an Irish writer could be successful without appearing under a London imprint. The book was published by William Curry (–1825–d.c.1870), who became a key figure in the publishing revival. The success of the *Dublin*

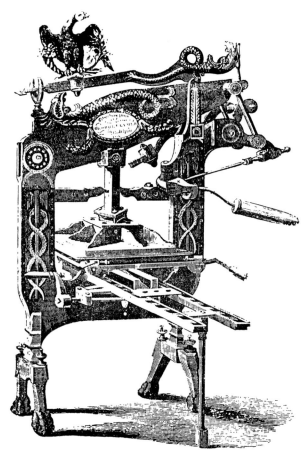

The Columbian Press, one of the most widely used printing presses of the nineteenth century.

University Magazine, founded in 1833 and which survived until
1877, making it the longest-running literary journal ever published
in Ireland, confirmed that the tide had turned. There was a
new confidence in the air. A recent study has shown that whereas
only 20 per cent of material in Irish periodicals in 1790 was
original, by 1830 this had risen to 90 per cent.

James Duffy (1809–1871) carried progress further in the
following decade, publishing many of the authors of the Young
Ireland Movement in his series *The Library of Ireland*. He specialised
in inexpensive nationalist literature, and in 1860 was large enough
to establish a London office. Also in the 1840s the long-established

The first steam printing press to be installed in Ireland by the *Dublin
Penny Journal* in 1834.

Belfast firm of Simms and M'Intyre emerged from being local printers and publishers to take on the British market with their revolutionary *Parlour Library* series of cheap fiction.

Parallel with these developments, from 1831 onwards, the Commissioners of National Education started to issue their national school books. Alexander Thom (1801–1879) was the principal printer employed. These books were a great change from the traditional school book and proved a huge success. Their phenomenal reception led to a large export trade, so much so that in 1850 some London publishers sought, unsuccessfully, to have their importation curtailed. In 1850 these books had 25 per cent of the English national schoolbook market; by 1859 that share had doubled.

The optimism in the book trades was reflected on the technical side. In the 1830s there was enough demand from printers for a Dublin engineer, Joseph Aldritt, to modify imported iron printing presses and market them as 'Alldritt's Improved Columbian Printing Press'. And in 1834 the first steam press in the country was installed by Philip Dixon Hardy, who used it to print the *Dublin Penny Magazine*.

The recovery of the book trade was interrupted by the devastations of the Great Famine of 1845–9, and some of the largest businesses in Dublin were bankrupted, including Milliken, Folds, Coyne, and Curry. The minute books of the DTPS record that in July 1847 journeymen in employment were required to pay seven times the normal subscription of six-pence to provide relief for the unemployed members of the trade.

Better communications in the second half of the century precipitated a decline in provincial presses. The improved postal service and the spread of the railway network following the

Railway Act of 1847 meant that the bigger towns could supply the printing needs of the outlying areas. Steamships plying the Irish Sea made it possible for London printers to provide partly-printed sheets to Irish newspapers, who would pass the sheets through their own presses, adding local news. The *Daily Express* in Dublin, the *Munster News* in Limerick, the *Waterford Mail*, and the *Ballina Herald* all availed of this service in 1860. Improved communications also proved a threat to Dublin's dominance of

University Printing Office as shown in the *Dublin Penny Journal* 10th October 1835. It was later named Dublin University Press.

the Irish wholesale book supply market. Belfast was able to get British publications from London, shipped through Fleetwood, and Cork and Waterford through Bristol. The improvements in communications, of course, also operated in opposite direction: Irish firms could print and publish for the British market and the colonies. James McGlashan (–c.1830–d.1858) published jointly with many of the larger British houses, and Michael Henry Gill (1794–1879), at the Dublin University Press, printed for many of them. Large printing and publishing houses could survive in the bigger cities, catering for the Irish and overseas markets. Marcus Ward and Co., established in Belfast in 1833, did a huge amount of business printing Vere Foster's copybooks for the international market. State-of-the-art chromo-lithography became one of its specialities. W. & G. Baird, founded in 1852, was another large Belfast printing house. It continues in existence today, as does Guy and Co., stationers and printers in Cork. Guys was started in the late 1840s. It was the first firm in Cork to have lithographic machine presses and by the early 1880s had grown to the extent that it employed over 100 workers.

The second half of the century was one of stability and consolidation. The census returns show the following figures for book trade employees:

	1841	*1851*	*1861*	*1871*
Printing	1,717	2,178	2,848	3,421
Bookselling	336	510	533	575

	1881	*1891*	*1901*
All Book Trades	7,112	7,722	8,122

There was not much movement in printers' conditions throughout the century. By an agreement of 1829 the compositors' piece rate in Dublin had advanced only a halfpenny per 1,000 ens from the scale of 4½d. in 1800. A working week of six ten hour days was the norm. Agitation for a further halfpenny per 1,000 ens and shorter hours began in 1869. During negotiations between the DTPS and the Master Printers it was pointed out that printers' wages had not advanced in forty years while general prices had increased 50 per cent. Newspaper compositors, the best paid in the trade, got only £1-10-0 per week. The increase of a halfpenny was granted by the book and jobbing printers in March 1870, but the newspaper houses refused to grant it.

It was patent that industrial peace would not last long. A memorial was presented to the employers in December 1877 seeking a range of increases, including a further halfpenny rise in the piece rate, an increase of 2 shillings on the 'stab' rate of 13 shillings, and a reduction of the working week to 54 hours. This was the first shot in a bitter struggle which included a nine-month strike that nearly crippled the DTPS. It began in March 1878 and the employers met it head-on by importing strike-breaking labour from England and Scotland. Some firms did pay increases and their men continued to work. However, the DTPS had to impose crippling levies on these men in an effort to pay something to the strikers. Many of these workers openly revolted and withheld the money. Loans were sought from other typographical societies to provide strike pay. In May the Society sent a printed memorial to every member of parliament asking for intervention and Parnell raised the matter in the House of Commons. And still the strike dragged on. By the start of Winter there was little fight left in the men. Defeated, they returned to work on 25 November, and all wages reverted to the pre-strike rates.

Advances in mechanisation were quickly assimilated by the DTPS. Its *Rules for Working Type Composing Machines* was issued in December 1886. In 1888, eight years after its invention, the *Freeman's Journal* was one of the first in Ireland to install the Thorne 'cold metal' typesetting machines. The Dublin Steam Printing Company had the honour of importing the first 'hot metal' Linotypes; it had them in operation by mid-1893, shortly after its invention. About 1880 Richard Wright in Dublin started producing his 'Emerald' presses, the first cylinder printing machines to be made in Ireland.

The Linotype hot metal typesetting machine first appeared in Dublin in 1893. Mechanical composition such as this and Monotype had a huge impact on print production.

The century ended with the printing and publishing trades in the doldrums of a general trade depression. Unemployment among printers was high, while publishers continued to be extremely cautious.

The Twentieth Century

THE depression continued into the new century. There was high unemployment among printers and several Irish publishers, Gills and Falconers among them, were sending books abroad to be printed. An early issue of the *Irish Printer* said that 1905 was 'probably one of the worst years that most printers can remember'. There was some hope that the revival of national spirit then underway in such movements as the Gaelic League, the Irish National Theatre and the Irish National Literary Society, would give rise to a vibrant literary publishing industry. The literary revival did spawn Maunsels (founded in 1906) and in some measure the Dun Emer Press (founded by Elizabeth Corbet Yeats in 1902 as part of a women's craft cooperative; it changed its name to the Cuala Press in 1908). But these were peripheral to the main trends.

The circumstances of the First World War gave rise to rapid economic inflation. There were huge rises in printing costs. The Dublin printers engaged in a series of lengthy strikes for better conditions. By the end of the war the basic printer's wage was £3, an increase of 70 per cent on its pre-war level. The working week had come down to 51 hours. And although some printers still worked on piece rates (which was officially abolished only in 1930), most worked on fixed wages. A weeks' annual leave was granted in 1919. Problems in the book trades were compounded by the destruction caused during the 1916 Rebellion. Maunsels was gutted, as was Easons, and Thoms was badly damaged (the plates for *Thom's Dublin Directory* were destroyed and it was feared it would never appear again).

The general economic depression continued after Independence in 1922. The Civil War in 1922–3 added to the general slump. Printers' basic wages in Dublin had inflated to £4–12–6 by 1920 and the working week reduced to 48 hours. The tables were turned in 1922 when employers forced a reduction to £4–4–0, the only time this reversal has happened in the industry.

The Dun Emer pressmark – wood engraving by
Elinor Monsell.

The Censorship of Publications Act (1926) tempered any adventurousness that publishers may have had. The dominant publishing houses were the Talbot Press, Duffys and Gills, whose output was a mixture of schoolbooks, light literature and Catholic piety. The Dundalgan Press in Dundalk was one of the few provincial houses doing any significant publication. Irish language publishing, buoyed up by state encouragement, could

33

afford to be more innovative. *An Gúm*, the government's imprint, was founded in 1926, and Sairséal agus Dill followed later, starting in 1947.

There were constant complaints in the trade literature throughout the 1920s about the high levels of imported printed matter. Protective tariffs were demanded and the Printing Trades Protection Committee was launched. Large printing houses were heavily dependent on government printing contracts. The imposition of import tariffs, increased to 75 per cent on printed matter in 1933 during the Economic War with Britain, led to a boom in the printing industry. The DTPS minutes of May 1931 record a 'recent avalanche of work'. Unemployed lists were cleared and overtime was constantly being worked. There were large imports of printing machinery to cope with the demand; Helys was to the fore in this regard. The Ludlow caster and the

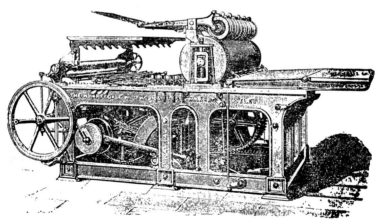

An early Wharfedale machine. It was the workhorse of the printing industry in the late nineteenth and early twentieth centuries.

Rotaprint press made their first appearances in Dublin in 1935. The number of employees in the industry increased from 4,353 to 4,966 between 1931 and 1935. But the demand was artificial and at the end of the Economic War in 1938 the industry was thrown back into recession. Unemployment among printers in 1939 was six times higher than in previous years.

The poor standards of typography in Irish publications was a recurrent complaint throughout the 1920s, '30s and '40s. 'The real trouble about most books published in Ireland...' wrote George Russell in a December 1926 issue of the *Irish Statesman,* 'is that they are utterly without taste...' F. R. Higgins later labelled the typography as 'the imprint of the cloven hoof'. Thomas Bodkin, Director of the National Gallery, caused a huge row in 1932 when he sent his book *Hugh Lane and his Pictures* abroad to be printed because he felt Ireland 'lacked the necessary plant and experienced craftsmen' to produce such an elaborate work. Colm O Lochlainn (1892–1972) replied that everything except the collotype plates could have been done in the country. O Lochlainn's Three Candles Press, founded in 1926, was one of the few beacons of good taste in Irish printing and publishing during this period. He also taught in the School of Printing, which was established in the Bolton Street Technical College in 1934. The launch of the Young Master Printers' Association in the late '30s helped, too, in raising standards.

The printing industry enjoyed something of a boom in the period of the Second World War and its aftermath, but for the publishers it was a time of stasis. The foundation of the Mercier Press in Cork in 1944, specialising in Catholic literature, was the exception. The home market for publishers was sluggish and exports to Great Britain were placed under a virtual embargo by British trade restrictions in the years 1947–1949. The small literary publishing house run by Michael Fridberg suffered particularly badly as Britain accounted for 87 per cent of his sales. It was a time for reflection by the Irish publishers. The potential value of the American and Australian markets was identified, but without marketing and distribution networks they remained impenetrable.

Colm O Lochlainn, founder of the Three Candles Press
and acknowledged as one of the finest printers in Dublin during the
early part of the twentieth century. (*courtesy Eamonn De Burca*)

In 1950, in the third issue of *Envoy*, John Ryan decried the fact that serious Irish authors still felt the need to go to London to be published. Liam Miller (1924–1987) founded the Dolmen Press in 1951 to provide an outlet for these authors, and over the following decades printed and published hundreds of their works. At the same time his high standards of typography lifted the design standards in the industry as a whole.

During the 1950s and '60s restrictive censorship continued to stifle any adventure among Irish publishers, and in the main the industry languished. The bulk of the output into the 1960s was insular in outlook – a perennial diet of schoolbooks, Catholic

Liam Miller, founder of the Dolmen Press
Etching by Jack Coughlin, 1976.

37

literature, and popular Irish authors. The recurrent need for textbooks meant that the educational houses weathered the period better than the general trade publishers. The amelioration of the Censorship Act in 1967 provided a beacon of hope for the industry.

In contrast, the printing trade was booming, riding the crest of industrial revival. Machines were idle only because of the shortage of trained printers. In 1961 printing was the Republic's fourth largest industry. Conditions had improved significantly for the printers: the magic 40 hour week was achieved in 1964 and the basic wage was nearly £15. Three weeks holiday was achieved in the following year. But already fears were being expressed about the effects of changes then happening in printing technology. Computer typesetting and offset-litho printing were beginning to displace the traditional letterpress technology. The full effects of these changes took place during the oil crises of the mid-1970s and led to several business failures and much industrial unrest. The massive economic turmoil can be judged by the fact that the basic printer's wage had been inflated to £50 by the end of 1975.

In 1974 one of the largest printing and publishing firms, Irish University Press in Shannon, which had specialised in the reprinting of the huge series of nineteenth-century British Parliamentary Papers, went bankrupt. Ironically its failure helped fuel the revival in Irish publishing, then underway. Several of its redundant staff went on to establish their own publishing houses – Irish Academic Press, Wolfhound, *Books Ireland* among them. At the same time the Blackstaff Press was founded in Belfast, to be followed a few years later by Appletree. It is estimated that the book market in Ireland increased 60 per cent between 1981 and 1985. In the 1980s the number of publishers increased by a third.

Proper marketing and distribution at home and abroad were always weaknesses of the Irish publishing industry. In 1970 Clé (the Irish Book Publishers' Association) was founded by seven publishing houses to fill the marketing gap. By the early '80s there were sixty members in the Association. In 1980 Irish Bookhandling was founded by some of the smaller publishers to provide centralised distribution and invoicing. Unfortunately financial irregularities led to its cessation in 1986. The lesson, however, had been learned, and Gill and Macmillan Distribution now handles the output of most Irish trade publishers.

The upturn in Irish publishing helped to lift the printing industry out of its recession. Irish printers have always been general jobbing houses; there was never enough work for specialist book printers. As a consequence Irish publishers, including the largest, Gill and Macmillan, continued to send commissions abroad where specialist book printers could provide a service up to 35 per cent cheaper than Irish printers, with much shorter delivery dates. By 1990 the expansion in the publishing industry was such that the first specialist book printer in the country, ColourBooks, could be launched.

There are three main reasons for the growth of Irish publishing over the past two decades: an increasingly well-educated population; the strengthening of the economy since Ireland joined the European Community in 1973; and changes in printing technology which allow for the economic production of the small editions that suit the Irish market.

ιοιρ Єιριηη αζυρ Ⅽlbαιη. bíoηη ρέ ρυαρ αζυρ ριαδάη αηηρυδ
ρα ραṁραδ ρέιη αζυρ ιρ· mιηιc α bíoηη ρ·coιρmeαċα móρα αηη.
Ní ραbαδαρ ι bραδ αηη ζο δτάιηιζ ρ·coιρm móρ υατbáραc αζυρ·
bí ραιτċíoρ móρ oρτα.

Ⅽ "Iρ ciηητe ζο ρcαραιδ αη ρ·coιρm ó céιle·ριηη" áρρα
Ⅎιoηηζυαlα "αċ τά α ριορ αζαιb Ⅽαρραιζ ηα Ⅰⱦóη. Ⲧιζιmíρ·
le céιle αηηριη ηυαιρ α béαρ αη ρ·coιρm ċαρτ."

Ⅽ Ⲛυαιρ α τάιηιζ αη ṁαιδιη ċυαιδ Ⅎιoηηζυαlα ι η-áιρδe αρ
Ⅽαρραιζ ηα Ⰽⱦóη αζυρ δ·ρéαċ ρí αmαċ αρ αη mυιρ ι ηζαċ áιρδ,
αċ ní ραιb le ρειceál αc ηα τoηητραċα móρα αζ léιmηιζ ι
η-áιρδe αζυρ αζ ριτ ι ηδιαιδ α céιle αζυρ αη cυbαρ báη αρ
nóρ ρηeαċτα αρ α mbáρρ. Ⅿαιδιη lá αρ ηα báραċ coηηαιc
ρí Ⅽoηη αζ τeαċτ ċuιce ζo lαζ τυιρρeαċ τηáιζτe. Ⅰⱦíoρ bραδα
ζo δτάιηιζ Ⅎιαċρα αζυρ ní ραιb αηη lαbαιρτ bí ρé ċoṁ cυρτα
ριη. Ⅾo ċυιρ Ⅎιoηηζυαlα αη beιρτ ραoι η-α δά ρcιατάη:"Ⅾά
mbéαδ Ⅽoδ αζαιηη αηoιρ" αρ ριρe, "beιmíρ ράρτα."

Ⅽ Ⲧαρ éιρ ταmαιll τάιηιζ Ⅽoδ αζυρ ċυιρ Ⅎιoηηζυαlα ραoι
ċleιτí α huċτα é. Ⅾ·ραηαδαρ mαρ ριη ζo ραιb αη τυιρρe
cυρτα δíob. Ⅽċ mo léαη! ιρ ιomδα oιδċe υατbáραċ mαρ ριη
δo bíoδ αcα ι ριτ ηα mblιαη ι η-α διαιδ ριη.

Ⅽ Ⅽċ τάιηιζ αoη oιδċe αṁáιη ι mí Єαηαιρ αζυρ αη αιmριρ
ηíoρ ρυαιρe ηá mαρ δo bí αoη oιδċe eιle ρoιṁe ριη ηá ι η-α,

A page from *Clann Lir* (Dublin 1922), printed in the Gaelic type
designed by George Petrie, artist, antiquary and musician. It is considered one of the most beautiful and formal of Irish typefaces and
was first cut around 1840.

SOURCES:

Pollard, Mary, *Dublin's Trade in Books 1550–1800*, Oxford 1989.

Phillips, James W., *Printing and Bookselling in Ireland, 1670–1800: A Bibliographical Enquiry*, Dublin 1998.

Munter, Robert, *A Dictionary of the Print Trade in Ireland 1550–1775*, New York 1988.

Kinane, Vincent, *A History of the Dublin University Press 1734–1976*, Dublin 1994.

Sessions, William K., *The First Printers in Waterford, Cork and Kilkenny pre-1700*, York 1990.

Wheeler, W. G., 'The Spread of Provincial Printing in Ireland up to 1850', *Irish Booklore* v. 4 no. 1 (1978) p. 7–19.

Adams, J. R. R., *The Printed Word and the Common Man: Popular Culture in Ulster 1700–1900*, Belfast 1987.

Long, Gerard ed., *Books Beyond the Pale: Aspects of the Provincial Book Trade in Ireland before 1850*, Dublin 1996.

Irish Print Union, Archives of the Dublin Typographical Provident Society, 1829 onwards (microfilm copy in the Department of Early Printed Books, Trinity College Library, Dublin).

Progress in Irish Printing, Dublin 1936.

Fishwick, F., *The Market for Books in the Republic of Ireland*, Dublin 1987.

Farmar, Tony, *A Brief History of Clé (the Irish Book Publishers' Association): 1970–1995*, Dublin 1995.

ABOUT THE AUTHOR

VINCENT KINANE

16 February 1953 – 30 November 2000

A Dubliner by birth and inclination, Vincent Kinane was educated at St. Mary's College, Rathmines, and University College Dublin. Soon after graduating in 1973 he joined the staff of Trinity College Library being first attached to the Readers' Services department but soon moving to the Department of Early Printed Books in 1974.

This department was to be his spiritual home for the rest of his life. He was vigorously schooled in historical bibliography by M. Pollard, then head of the department. His interest in Irish printing, particularly of the eighteenth century developed swiftly. This interest became more closely focussed on the Dublin University Press, sparked off, perhaps, by the proceeds of several salvage expeditions to the College Printing House in the wake of the departure of the Dublin University Press from the premises in 1976. The department's own handpress, Trinity Closet Press, moved into the basement of the Printing House. These events led to his examination of the eighteenth-century records of the Dublin University Press for a fellowship of the Library Association of Ireland and later to his book, *A History of the Dublin University Press 1734–1976,* published in 1994. A by-product of his research was the donation of several volumes of records of the firm to the College by Michael Gill.

Producing Trinity Closet Press's annual publications on an Alexandra hand press developed his interest in typography and made him an obvious choice for membership of the editorial committee of the *Treasures of the Library Trinity College Dublin* published in 1986 and also the obvious successor to W. E. Mackey as editor of *Long Room* in 1991. He filled this office with distinction, enlarging the appeal and scope of the journal. He was the instigator, and joint editor with Anne Walsh, of *Essays on the History of Trinity College Library* published in 2000. This was the first large scale survey of the library as an institution examining aspects of its operation over four centuries.

His research and publications, and his achievements as an editor were all done in spare time after the day's work in the department. He made a great contribution to the reputation of the department both by scholarly advice to readers and in developing the collection. His greatest enthusiasms were for the novel and fine bookbindings. In the first he had the task of trying to redress the cavalier attitude of nineteenth-century librarians and was tireless in pursuit of new titles for the collection. His interest in fine bindings is reflected in several purchases made for the library and the better preservation of many items already in the collection. It also led to his secondment to manage the Worth Library in Dr. Steevens's Hospital. This gem of about 4,000 volumes in superb condition remains in the room constructed for it in 1734 and was reliant on the catalogue produced at that time. His task was to catalogue it to modern standards. He succeeded only in cataloguing one third of it before his death but he laid the foundation for a masterly study of the bindings commissioned by Edward Worth in the early decades of the eighteenth century. The work when completed will be a significant contribution to the history of the Irish booktrade.

ABOUT THE TYPEFACE

This old face design, Bembo 270, has such an up-to-date appearance that it is difficult to realise this letter was cut before 1500. At Venice in 1495, Aldus Manutius Romanus printed a small 36 page tract, *Petri Bembi de Aetna ad Angelum Chabrielem liber,* written by the young humanist poet Pietro Bembo (later Cardinal, and Secretary to Pope Leo X), using a new design of type. The punches were cut by Francesco Griffo of Bologna, the designer responsible six years later for the first italic types.

An The
Chomhairle Heritage
Oidhreachta Council

ACKNOWLEDGEMENT

This publication was grant-aided by The Heritage Council under their Publication Grant Scheme in 2002.

The National Print Museum was officially opened by President Mary Robinson on the 3rd April 1996. It is housed in the old garrison chapel in Beggars Bush, Dublin 4. On display are a wide variety of printing and typesetting machines from the days of letterpress and hot metal. Much of the equipment is in working order and the museum hosts festivals of printing each year.

47